Good Tidings Of Great Joy

Six Advent Dramas

Cynthia S. Baker

CSS Publishing Company, Inc
Lima, Ohio

GOOD TIDINGS OF GREAT JOY

Scripture quotations are from the *New Revised Standard Version of the Bible,* copyright 1989 by the Division of Christian Education of the National Council of the Churches of Christ in the USA. Used by permission

This book is available in the following formats, listed by ISBN:
0-7880-0097-7 Book

PRINTED IN U S A

To my husband John, dearest and best —
for his thoughtful criticism,
constant encouragement,
and unfailing love.

Table of Contents

Production Notes

Settings

Can be very simple. A plain neutral background would suffice.

Properties

A few chairs or stools; a cashbox for the innkeeper's wife.

Costumes

Ideas can be gathered from religious Christmas cards. Soldier should have short tunic, sandals, short red cloak. Helmet and sword are effective additions, if they can be located. Theater supply houses often have paper mache helmets. Gabriel, being "in disguise," could wear almost anything.

Advent Introduction

(The section between the asterisks is optional.)

(Enter Narrator and Reader.)

*

Narrator: The little nation of Israel, chosen by God to bear witness of him to the world, had been suffering for 400 years for their disobedience and rebellion against God. They had been conquered, taken into bondage, and had suffered servitude under Assyria, and Egypt, and Syria, and finally Rome. And during the 400 years, there had been no prophet of the Lord, no voice to lift them up. The hope they clung to was in the ancient scrolls, in the words of the prophets of God who had lived during the last days of the kingdom of Judah, and who had warned them of coming disaster. But even in their prophecies of doom, these prophets had also left a ray of hope, and a promise from God. Foremost among these was the prophet Isaiah.

Reader: "I will wait for the Lord, who is hiding his face from the house of Jacob, and I will hope in him ... in the former time he brought into contempt the land of Zebulun and the land of Naphtali, but in the latter time he will make glorious the way of the sea, the land beyond the Jordan, Galilee of the nations" (Isaiah 8:17; 9:1).

Narrator: The people wanted to believe that God would send them a warrior king, like King David, who would restore the glory of the nation of Israel.

Reader: "The people who walked in darkness have seen a great light; those who lived in a land of deep darkness — on them light has shined" (Isaiah 9:2). . . . "For a child has been born for us, a son given to us; and authority rests upon his shoulders, and he is named Wonderful Counselor, Mighty God, Everlasting Father, Prince of Peace" (Isaiah 9:6).

Narrator: But Isaiah spoke also of a suffering Messiah, one who would not sit on a throne but be stretched upon a cross to pay for their sins; one who would teach righteousness and holy living, but who would be misunderstood; one who would heal the blind and the lame, but who would be rejected by the people he came to save. Nobody wanted to think about that. They went on hoping for what they wanted; and no one was really prepared for any of the things that came to pass when, in the fullness of time, the Messiah finally came.

*

Narrator: When our Lord Jesus was born, as we all know and have been told many times, he was not born in a hospital. He was not even born at home. His young mother delivered her baby in a strange town, in a stable, on a bed of straw. Few of us who are mothers would have welcomed such circumstances — and it seems strange to us that this was what God had ordained for his most precious and only Son. But as always, God knew exactly what he was doing.

Lives of many people were touched by Jesus' birth; indeed, lives were altered and redirected even before his birth, because of him. We do not know who all of them were, but we can imagine what contact with this strangely wonderful event might have meant to some of them. In doing this, we have elaborated on the simple biblical narrative; so we ask that you remember that ONLY the words of scripture bear the weight of God's inspired message to us.

Let us begin with Mary, a godly young peasant woman of Nazareth, serenely happy and engaged to be married, whose life was completely turned upside down by the plans of God. Hear the words of God, as we find them in Luke 1:26-34:

Reader: *(Reads Luke 1:26-34.)*

(Reader sits down on stage.)

Narrator: When Mary did find herself pregnant, we can imagine that she must have found it difficult to explain the circumstances to her family, and to Joseph, her fiance. We do know from the scriptures that she fled for understanding to her cousin Elizabeth, who, the angel had told her, was also pregnant — another of God's miracles, for Elizabeth was both old and barren. Hear the words of God as we find them in Luke 1:39-45, and verse 56:

Reader: *(Reads Luke 1:39-45, and verse 56.)*

(Reader sits.)

Narrator: So we know from the Bible record that Mary stayed with Elizabeth for three months, returning to Nazareth just before the birth of Elizabeth's baby, who would be known as John the Baptist. We can imagine that this time together was very precious to both women. Let us listen in on a conversation that might have taken place as Mary was getting ready to leave.

(Exit Narrator and Reader.)

11

Mary And Elizabeth

(Enter Mary and Elizabeth, stage left.)

Elizabeth: Do you have all your things together for the journey, Mary?

Mary: I think so.

Elizabeth: Then come, let us sit down and have one more talk. These last few minutes are very precious to me, Mary. I can hardly bear to see you go.

Mary: Oh, Elizabeth! What am I going to do without you! You have been the one person to whom I could open my whole heart during these difficult days! Even Joseph, dear as he is, cannot comprehend what it is really like for me.

Elizabeth: And you have been a wonderful comfort to me, dear heart. Poor Zechariah! Struck dumb by the angel, and unable to talk all these many months — we cannot converse without the tedious procedure of having him write down all his responses. And being a man, he can't put anything intimate in writing without a gigantic struggle!

(They both laugh a little.)

Mary: I wish I didn't have to leave quite yet. I still have many months of pregnancy to go, and it seems like an eternity.

Elizabeth: It is best that we not flout tradition, Mary. You know that it is not considered suitable for a virgin to be present when a child is born. Of course, your situation is very special. None of our neighbors would accept the fact that you are a virgin, in view of your condition, but you and I know it. And I can tell that my time for the birth is very near.

Mary: You are right, of course. It wouldn't be any easier to leave then than it is now, anyway. And I must admit I do long to see Joseph again. It's just that the gossipy women of Nazareth can be so unkind! Inside, I feel so special, so blessed by God, so full of a beautiful joy — and they can make my situation seem so sordid, and dirty, and wrong. I wish THEY had been struck dumb, instead of Zechariah!

Elizabeth: You won't have to put up with it much longer, Mary. Zechariah had a communication for me last night, from the ancient prophecies. You know the scriptures, but you may not have given much thought to this one. Your baby won't be born in Nazareth.

Mary: Not born in Nazareth! What do you mean? The angel didn't say anything about that!

Elizabeth: The angel didn't need to. It's all in the written word of God. Listen — this is what Zechariah copied out of the scroll for you:

(She brings out a small scroll and reads from it.)

> "But you, O Bethlehem, who are one of the little clans of Judah, from you shall come forth for me one who is to rule in Israel, whose origin is from of old, from ancient days" (Micah 5:2).

14

You see? And your little one will be ruler in Israel, for so the angel said. And he is the Son of God, whose origin is from old, from ancient days.

Mary: Bethlehem! How on earth am I to get to Bethlehem?

Elizabeth: If the Lord wants you in Bethlehem, he'll get you there. But Zechariah thinks he knows how it will come about. You know that he hears all kinds of rumors in the temple? Well, the latest one is that Caesar is considering a new census, as the basis for a new tax; and that he will require people to register in their ancestral cities. For Joseph, because he is of the house of David, this will mean a trip to Bethlehem. And when he goes, you must go with him. God will take care of the rest.

Mary: Bethlehem! It is a whole new idea to me. I have heard the old prophecies, of course. I just hadn't thought about it until now. I had thought that of course my mother and my neighbors would be with me.

Elizabeth: Is the idea so hard to accept?

Mary: As I think about it — no, not really. There are times when Mother's reproachful looks are as hard to take as the neighbors' gossip. She has never accepted my story about the angel. She and Father think the baby is Joseph's.

(She stands up, suddenly exultant.)

God is good! There is really great comfort in that thought! I am strong and healthy — I can endure the journey if we go slowly. And dear Joseph will be there, and we will be alone and together, praise the Lord! God will provide for his little Son! Oh, Elizabeth, thank you! Now I believe I really have the courage to go home!

(There is a rapping at the door.)

15

Elizabeth: Yes, and the time has come. That will be the servant at the door with the donkey. You are dearer to me than a daughter could have been, Mary! May God's blessings go with you always!

Mary: Farewell, dearest Elizabeth!

(They embrace.)

This time with you has meant more than I can ever say. Joseph and I will be eager to hear about the birth of your little son. Farewell!

(Exit Mary, stage left. Elizabeth stands looking after her.)

Elizabeth: She is gone. Dear Mary! There is a great deal ahead for both of us that will be difficult — yet of all women, we are most blessed. And whatever befalls, God will see us through.

(Exit Elizabeth, stage right.)

The Villagers
Of Nazareth

Narrator: The gospel writer Luke tells us that "in those days, a decree went out from Caesar Augustus that all the world should be enrolled" (Luke 2:1). Did you ever wonder how people got the word? No newspapers, no television, no telephones. They sent messengers, usually soldiers, in sufficient strength to deal with any hostile demonstrations. The announcement in the village of Nazareth might have gone something like this:

(Exit Narrator.)

Scene 1: *A street in Nazareth. Three Villagers (either male or female) enter casually, from both sides of the stage. Mary and Joseph also enter, and mingle. If desired, stage setting can include a village well, and the women can be carrying water jars on their heads, and simulate filling them at the well (optional). There is the sound of a trumpet, and villagers all crowd together on stage left as a Roman Soldier enters, stage right. He is caped and helmeted, wearing a sword. He carries a scroll.*

Roman Soldier: People of Nazareth, attend me!

(Villagers look at each other, murmuring; then look back at the soldier, and are silent.)

17

Roman Soldier: I am ordered by His Imperial Highness, Caesar Augustus, to deliver the following imperial decree: that all the peoples of his empire shall go to be enrolled, each one to his own city, without exception, and without delay. Hear ye all, and see to it!

1st Villager: *(to 2nd Villager)* We all know what that means — more taxes!

2nd Villager: Hush! He'll hear you!

3rd Villager: *(loudly, to soldier)* How can we be expected to leave our flocks and herds? Surely someone must remain behind!

1st Villager: I have no money for such a journey. It took all I had to pay the last tax!

2nd Villager: My aged father has been bedridden for over a year, and cannot travel at all!

Roman Soldier: *(angrily)* Imperial commands require obedience — not complaints! You will feel the full weight of Roman justice if you disobey!

(Exit Roman Soldier, stage right.)

3rd Villager: *(bitterly)* Roman justice! Bah! I spit upon Roman justice!

2nd Villager: Be quiet, can't you? You'll get us all in trouble!

3rd Villager: He's gone.

2nd Villager: You know as well as I do that the very walls have ears! Mind your tongue.

1st Villager: *(to Joseph)* You are very silent, Joseph. Have you nothing to say about this new outrage?

Joseph: I am no happier about this than any of you. It means that I must travel all the way from Nazareth to the city of Bethlehem in Judea, because I am of the house and lineage of David. I would not mind for myself, but Mary will have to go with me, and the trip will be both hard and dangerous for her, so close to the time when her baby will be born.

1st Villager: This is true. You have my sympathy.

2nd Villager: And mine.

3rd Villager: *(angrily, shaking his fist at the sky)* If only we had a leader, a champion to help us overthrow this detestable Roman government!

2nd Villager: Angry words won't change anything. We all know what we must do. I am going to get ready for the journey.

(Exit, stage left.)

1st Villager: Me too.

(Exit, stage left.)

3rd Villager: I didn't say I wouldn't go — wait for me!

(Exit, stage left.)

Joseph: Mary, how can we possibly go now, with the birth of your baby so near?

Mary: I am not afraid. Joseph, don't you remember that according to the words of the Prophet Micah, the Messiah will come forth from Bethlehem? Caesar Augustus may think this new enrollment is his own idea; but it may very well be the will of God. If it is his will that his son be born in Bethlehem, we can be sure he will take care of us. Let us make ready.

19

Joseph: You are right, of course. We will travel slowly, with great care.

(Exeunt, stage right.)

The
Innkeeper's Wife

Narrator: The scriptures tell us very little about the arrival of Joseph and Mary in Bethlehem. We know that all the people of the house and lineage of David were required to go to Bethlehem to be enrolled, so it is not hard to imagine how crowded the little town must have been. The record simply states that Mary "gave birth to her firstborn son and wrapped him in bands of cloth, and laid him in a manger, because there was no place for them in the inn" (Luke 2:7). But someone saw their need, and made it possible for them to stay in the stable. Let us imagine a sympathetic innkeeper's wife, and what the encounter might have meant to her.

(Exit Narrator.)

(Enter Innkeeper's Wife, wearing mob cap and apron, carrying a ledger. She sits down at a small table, and heaves a big sigh.)

Innkeeper's Wife: There! Finally, all the guests are quiet, for a change. What a tumult! All the rooms full — travellers even sleeping on the floors, rolled up in their mantles. And people still beating on the door, demanding that we put them up for the night. Well, no more tonight. No space — no space at all!

(She opens the ledger.)

Lucas will be pleased. We have never had this many paying guests before — and nothing pleases him quite so much as watching the silver pour in. As for me — well, I would trade the whole contents of the moneybox to change places with the young woman in the stable, sleeping with her newborn son in the curve of her arm.

(She closes the ledger, and rests her elbows on the table, with her chin in her hands.)

I was ashamed to put them in the stable — such a nice couple, country folks I would guess, and from the north, by their accent. The woman looked so dreadfully tired, and she was already having birthing pains; her young husband was just desperate to find a place for her. What else could I do? My rooms were all full; the stable was the only thing I could think of. But they were so grateful that I was embarrassed. I hope Lucas doesn't find out that I didn't charge them the full room rate. After all — a stable isn't a room, is it? It was a mercy there was plenty of loose straw to make a bed.

(She gets up and begins to walk up and down.)

But then — I no sooner got them settled than the baby began to come, so of course, I ran next door for the midwife; I've never had children, and I wasn't much help, but I hovered around, and fetched and carried, and did what I could. The birth was easy, praises be — and the child was just beautiful! The mother had come prepared with swaddling clothes, so we wrapped the little thing up — such a perfect little boy — and as I handed him to her, I told her how I had longed for a child myself, being married 15 years, and childless.

(She stops pacing, and speaks directly to the audience.)

22

Then — the strangest thing! The young mother sat up, looking right into my eyes, and said, "Place your hand on the baby's garments, and pray for a child of your own!" And I did! I went down on my knees, right on the dirty stable floor, laid my hand on that warm little squirming bundle, and stammered out a prayer, with the tears rolling down my cheeks.

(She takes out her handkerchief, and blows her nose.)

You probably think me mad, but for the first time in years, I have hope. I feel a fierce joy burning inside me. It is the most blessed thing I have ever done, helping that young couple — and I believe, I truly believe, that God himself has touched me. I, too, will have a baby — I KNOW I will! Praise the Lord!

(In a quieter, more normal voice.)

But, in the meantime, there are still a few last minute things to be done before I can sleep. *(Picks up the ledger.)* Money to count — see that the bars are on the doors —

(She starts exiting, still counting things off on her fingers.)

— set out Lucas' clean clothes for the morning — check the mousetraps in the kitchen — put the cat out —

(Her voice trails off as she exits.)

Ziph The Shepherd
And His Wife Jerah

Narrator: Luke's account of the birth of Jesus also tells us about some humble shepherds, who had perhaps the most fantastic birth announcement of all.

(At this point, if desired, Reader can read Luke 2:8-20.)

Let us assume that these shepherds might have had wives — and that, as they received the story secondhand from their husbands, it might have been difficult to believe. Let us further assume that even more might have happened than the scriptures record.

(Exit Narrator.)

(Enter Jerah, middle-aged peasant woman, poorly dressed. She keeps glancing offstage left, as though waiting for someone. She walks back and forth a few times — finally looks at the audience.)

Jerah: What am I doing here, you ask? I'm doing what I spend half my life doing — waiting for my husband. My name is

Jerah, and I'm the wife of Ziph, the shepherd. You probably won't recognize my name, but you must know Ziph. EVERYBODY knows Ziph. He's what you call a colorful character. *(Pause. She sighs.)*

Do you have ANY IDEA what it's like, to be married to a colorful character? Well, I won't go into detail, but it can be depressing at times.

(She glances offstage left again; then turns to the audience as if someone had asked her a question.)

What's that? You DON'T know Ziph? All right, I'll tell you about him.

(She pulls up a chair, and sits down facing the audience.)

Ziph is an old soldier, crippled in one leg from an old spear wound. Taking care of sheep is all he's good for now. He is well-known in Bethlehem, because he has a ready tongue, and an endless supply of stories, many of which have grown fat in the telling. He also has a bottomless thirst for wine, which has kept us in desperate poverty. I suspect that even now, he's at the inn, soaking it up.

(She looks offstage again.)

In fairness to him, I will say that he was first driven to the wine by the unbearable pain of his wound. Now it has a hold on him, and he can't shake it. But it's hard on me, I can tell you. I lose patience.

(She looks offstage again, and stands up, pushing back her chair.)

Well! Here comes my wandering sinner now!

(She takes an aggressive stance, with hands on hips, or arms folded.)

26

(Enter Ziph, stage left. He is poorly dressed, but neither drunk nor limping. He seems excited.)

Jerah: Well, it's about time! Where on earth have you been?

Ziph: Jerah! Just wait till I tell you!

Jerah: Now before you get started, I don't want to hear some long, cockeyed story. Are you drunk again?

Ziph: *(proudly)* Not a drop! Truly!

Jerah: Then why are you so late? A straight answer, now. I told you — I'm not interested in some wild story.

Ziph: Well, it IS a wild story, only — It's true! But if you won't listen, then just look!

(He walks back and forth a few times, pauses, and looks at Jerah as if waiting for a reaction. She says nothing.)

Ziph: All right then, look here!

(He jumps a few times, does a few leg exercises, looking at her expectantly.)

Jerah: *(Suddenly getting it.)* Ziph! Your leg! You're not limping!

Ziph: I not only am not limping, my dear wife — I am jumping for joy! NOW will you listen to my story?

Jerah: *(She has gone closer, and is leaning over, looking at his leg.)* But that's impossible! How many years has it been —

Ziph: JERAH!

Jerah: All right, all right — I'll listen.

(They pull up a couple of chairs, and sit, facing three-quarters toward audience, one-quarter toward each other.)

27

Ziph: Last night, as usual, Nemuel and Jether and I were out on the hills outside Bethlehem, tending our three flocks. We had made an enclosure for them out of thorn bushes, and all the sheep were inside and bedded down. The three of us were huddled around a little fire, trying to keep warm, when suddenly a bright light shone down on us, and a shining figure, larger than a man, stood there before us!

Jerah: And how many drinks had you had?

Ziph: Not one — as God is my witness!

Jerah: So, what happened next? Did the figure speak?

Ziph: We threw ourselves flat on the ground in terror — but the angel (that's what it was, an angel!) told us not to be afraid. He had a message for us.

Jerah: Oh, come on, Ziph! I'm trying to listen, but you're making it pretty hard! You're telling me that an angel made a special trip from heaven to give a message to three scruffy Bethlehem shepherds? Really, now!

Ziph: *(stubbornly)* That's exactly what I'm telling you. Do you want to know what happened, or don't you?

Jerah: I want you to get to the part about your leg.

Ziph: I'm getting there!

Jerah: *(resignedly)* All right. Go on. What did this angel say?

Ziph: He told us not to be afraid — that he had come with good news: that the Messiah, the Savior of Israel, had just been born in Bethlehem; that we were to go there and see, and we would find the young family in a stable, with the baby lying in a manger.

Jerah: In a MANGER! The Messiah in a manger?

Ziph: In a manger. That was to be our sign. And then, Jerah, the sky seemed suddenly to split apart — and for just a moment or two, there were thousands upon thousands of angels, praising God, blowing trumpets, and shouting, "Glory to God in the highest, and on earth, peace to men with whom he is pleased" (Luke 2:14).

Then, as quickly as it came, it all disappeared. The night was just as black, and ordinary, and quiet as usual. If ONLY ONE of us had seen it, we might have thought it was a dream — but we ALL saw it. So we hastened off to Bethlehem, to see if we could find this baby.

Nemuel and Jether were so excited they were almost running. I did my best, but of course I could only limp along, and I fell behind; but I managed to catch up with them when they reached the inn. Jether went in to inquire of the innkeeper's wife, and she directed us to the stable of the inn.

Sure enough! There were people in the stable, a young mother lying on a bed of hay, and a man at the entrance, who didn't want to let us in, at first. But when we told him about the angels, he said we could see the baby. We were trying to be quiet, but in the dark, I fell over a pitchfork and landed in a heap right beside the manger.

Jerah: The one with the baby in it?

Ziph: That's right. When I pulled myself up off the floor onto my knees, I was at eye level with the baby. And he opened his eyes, and looked right at me.

(He walks back and forth a few times with his head down, as if wondering just how to say what he wants to say.)

You know how unfocused babies' eyes are, when they're tiny? Well, this one actually seemed to see me. I put out one finger and touched his little hand — and suddenly, a sort of

29

burning tingle ran from my finger down my arm, and through my body, and down my bad leg. It felt the way I've always thought lightning might feel — what a shock!

At first, I thought I was being punished for daring to touch this holy child. But when I stood up, I found that my leg was healed —

(He moves, and flexes his leg.)

— and that for the first time in 20 years, I could move without pain! I couldn't believe it.

We stayed only a few minutes. I babbled out some sort of thanks — I really don't know what I said, and I don't think anybody knew what I was driving at, because of course I didn't look any different.

But when we came out of the stable, and I told Nemuel and Jether what had happened, and showed them what I could do, they were amazed too. The three of us ran around town like crazy men, telling everybody we met about all that had happened. I'm afraid most of them didn't believe us. Like you, Jerah.

Jerah: Yes — like me. But be fair, Ziph. Without the evidence of your healed leg — well, it's a lot to believe, and your reputation as a teller of tall tales is against you.

Ziph: But you believe me now?

Jerah: I believe you. Do you suppose I could go to see the little Messiah myself? We could take a birth gift. We don't have much, but there's my woolen shawl — and we could take a little goat cheese, and some apples.

Ziph: Fine — wonderful!

(They start moving off stage left as they talk.)

Ziph: I feel so good, Jerah — as if life is just beginning for me, for us. The world is going to be a very different place, now that the Messiah has come.

(Exeunt, stage left.)

Gabriel

Narrator: The birth of God's Son Jesus, the Savior and ultimately the King of humankind, represented a most wonderful bursting through of the divine presence into the lives of men. It was the high point in God's master plan. The Bible tells us that both men and angels were involved; and it even names the very special angel whose mission it was to convey God's messages to the people God had chosen. It isn't too difficult to imagine that even an archangel might have been excited.

(Exit Narrator. Enter Gabriel.)

Gabriel: *(impressively)* Behold! *(pause)* I am the Archangel Gabriel!
　　(In a more normal voice.) All right — so I don't look like your idea of an archangel. That's because I'm in disguise. If I came in here in all my power and glory, I guarantee you would all be flat on your faces with terror. When I appear as I really am, with a message to mortals from Almighty God, I always have to begin by telling them not to be afraid.
　　As God's favorite messenger, I've had some pretty interesting assignments. I'd rather have my job than Michael's. He's

33

an archangel too — I'm sure you know that — but he's the fighting angel, commander of God's legions, except when the Lord himself takes charge.

In most cases, the messages I bring to mankind are indications of God's special favor. I did the special effects on the burning bush that attracted Moses' attention, when he was tending his father-in-law's sheep in Midian — although God himself did the speaking that time, out of the fire.

I walked in the fiery furnace with Shadrach, Meshach and Abednego, and kept them from getting burned.

When Daniel was in the lion's den, I was the one who came and closed the lions' mouths. I appeared a number of times to Daniel, for he was a man greatly beloved.

But my favorite experiences were those connected with the birth of our Lord Jesus. It's not often I get to do birth announcements — although I was with the Lord that time he appeared to Abraham, and told him he would father a child in his old age.

Zechariah the priest wasn't quite as old as Abraham had been, but he was old enough so that he had given up all hope of children. When I burst upon him in the temple, beside the altar, he was terrified at first — a very appropriate reaction, as I have told you. I wasn't shining enough to blind him, but still, I was looking very splendid. I gave him the message from God very proudly. It was a wonderful message, about how he and Elizabeth his wife would become parents of a boy to be named John, who would grow up in the spirit and power of Elijah, and would preach repentance to the people of Israel, to prepare them for the coming of God's Son Jesus, the Savior.

And you know what? He didn't believe me! ME, Gabriel, archangel, straight from the presence of the Almighty! If you can't trust an archangel, whom can you trust?

I was so irritated that I struck the old man dumb, and told him he wouldn't be able to talk until after his son was born. (Let that be a lesson to you — never irritate an angel!)

After dealing with Zechariah, I waited about six months, and then had the privilege of making an appearance to Mary, the maiden chosen by God to be mother of the Christ child. She was so young — little more than a child herself. I admit I was more gentle and patient with Mary than I had been with Zechariah. After all, the word from God to her was a real stunner — that she, a betrothed virgin, was to bear the child of God. But after the first shock, she took it very well, with a quiet dignity unusual in one so young. I was proud of her. It was all I could do to refrain from patting her on the head.

My final encounter with humankind connected with the birth of Jesus was to appear to a group of very humble Bethlehem shepherds. They were scared out of their wits when I came blazing down to their hillside with my tidings of great joy. We angels were all very excited that night, for it was the birthnight of the Lord Jesus. And after I gave my message, telling them of the Lord's birth, and where to find him, I was permitted to draw back the curtain of sky and give them a glimpse of the hosts of heaven, shouting hallelujahs and playing their trumpets and harps. It was glorious — but of course it only lasted a few seconds. Then we withdrew, and the night was dark and silent again.

Those shepherds may not have been much to look at, but they didn't have any trouble believing the word, or obeying it, either. They went scrambling off to Bethlehem like so many scared rabbits.

And how about you, all of you? Do you believe? *(Warningly, shaking his finger at audience.)* Remember Zechariah — I don't want to have to get tough with you —

(Sound of bell — Gabriel looks up.)

What's that, Lord? Oh. Sorry.

(To audience.)

Let me rephrase that. I ENCOURAGE you with all my heart to believe. I will give you the heavenly message just as I gave it to the shepherds. The rest is up to you:

35

"For see — I am bringing you good news of great joy for all the people: to you is born this day in the city of David a Savior who is the Messiah, the Lord ... Glory to God in the highest heaven, and on earth peace among those whom he favors!" (Luke 2:10, 11, 14).

And do you want to be among those with whom God is pleased? Then believe! Receive the Lord of Christmas into your hearts this day, and the peace of God will be yours.

Farewell!

The Wise Men

(Enter Narrator.)

Narrator: The scriptures according to Matthew give us more details about the birth of Jesus not found in the Gospel of Luke. Not only the humble shepherds were told of the coming of the Messiah, but wise men who studied the stars in a distant country were also informed in quite a different way.
Here is the story as Matthew tells it:

(Enter Reader.)

Reader: *(Reads Matthew 2:1-12.)*

(Exit Reader.)

Narrator: We know that the arrival of the wise men took place some time after the visit by the shepherds, because they set out on their journey after they saw the star which proclaimed Jesus' birth. We don't know how long it took them, but Matthew stated that Mary and Joseph were in a house, and he called Jesus a child rather than a baby. Let us listen to a conversation that MIGHT have occurred between two of the wise men after they had seen the child Jesus.

(Exit Narrator.)

(Enter Caspar and Melchior.)

Caspar: Melchior, where is Balthazar?

Melchior: He is supervising the loading of the camels for our return journey.

Caspar: Have you given thought to our route? You know that King Herod practically commanded us to return to Jerusalem with word about the whereabouts of the little King — but I for one have no desire to go back that way. I had a strange dream last night, and I woke convinced that we should go a different way.

Melchior: Odd that you should say that — I had a dream, too! I am convinced that Herod has no desire to worship the child — he sees him as a threat to his throne. That would mean death to the child and his family if he knew where to find them.

Caspar: Then we are agreed. What about Balthazar?

Melchior: He may have had the same dream, although he has not mentioned it. He did tell me, though, that he feels we should avoid Jerusalem, and that we should make all possible haste to get out of the country. As long as we stay in Bethlehem, we are a danger to the little King, for I am certain Herod will have sent spies to follow us.

Caspar: Then we should certainly warn Joseph and Mary to leave town with their baby! Did you mention it to them?

Melchior: I tried. Joseph is aware that there is danger, but he is convinced that if he is to flee, God will tell him so, and will also say where he is to go. Even Nazareth, where they have been living, is not beyond Herod's reach.

Caspar: They would have been safer if we had never come!

Melchior: You know better than that, Caspar! Why do you think the Almighty God showed us the star? It was a summons — we were told to come!

Caspar: Well, it was certainly a mistake to go to Jerusalem!

Melchior: Yes, I admit that. When we came close to the city of Jerusalem, we stopped following the star and asked for directions. We should have just kept going, and never spoken to Herod at all.

Caspar: Too late for that now. All we can do is leave as rapidly as possible, and try to leave no trail. When Herod finds we have tricked him, he will be furious — his rages are well known. Our lives also would hang in the balance if he could get his hands on us.

Melchior: That is true. Let's check with Balthazar. He had the camels almost loaded. We can probably leave within the hour.

Caspar: Yes, let us go. We can say prayers for the little King and his parents on the way.

(Exeunt Caspar and Melchior.)

(Enter Narrator.)

Narrator: So the wise men, who had followed a star to Bethlehem, obeyed the dreams sent by God, and departed to their own country without reporting to Herod.

And scripture tells us that Joseph also received a warning dream, and the little family made their escape before the wrath of Herod descended on Bethlehem. Hear the words of God as recorded in Matthew 2:13-16:

(Enter Reader.)

Reader: *(Reads Matthew 2:13-16.)*

Narrator: And in Egypt also, Joseph was guided by dreams:

Reader: *(Reads Matthew 2:19-23.)*

Narrator: This concludes the story of the advent of Jesus, our Savior and our Lord, into the world of men. It was a life-changing event for those who were touched by it; and it can be a life-changing event for you also. Let us worship — like the wise men. Let us rejoice — like the shepherds. Let us receive — like the innkeeper's wife. Let us believe, and obey — like Mary and Joseph and Elizabeth. We must not forget, in our fascination with the baby in the manger, who that baby became.

Reader: *(Reads Isaiah 9:6-7.)*

Narrator: Let us all sing together "Joy To The World, The Savior Reigns."

(Exeunt.)

www.ingramcontent.com/pod-product-compliance
Lightning Source LLC
Chambersburg PA
CBHW071753020426
42331CB00008B/2301